Benjamin Br

Songs & Proverbs of William Blake

FOR BARITONE AND PIANO

OP. 74

FABER MUSIC LIMITED

3 Queen Square London

© 1965 by Faber & Faber Ltd
First published in 1965 by Faber & Faber Ltd
This edition published in 1977 by Faber Music Ltd
3 Queen Square London WC1N 3AU
Cover design by M & S Tucker
Printed in England

For Dieter:

the past and the future.

Proverb I
The pride of the peacock is the glory of God.
The lust of the goat is the bounty of God.
The wrath of the lion is the wisdom of God.
The nakedness of woman is the work of God.

LONDON

I wander thro' each charter'd street,
Near where the charter'd Thames does flow
And mark in every face I meet
Marks of weakness, marks of woe.

In every cry of every Man,
In every Infant's cry of fear,
In every voice, in every ban,
The mind-forg'd manacles I hear.

How the Chimney-sweeper's cry
Every black'ning Church appalls,
And the hapless Soldier's sigh
Runs in blood down Palace walls.

But most thro' midnight streets I hear
How the youthful Harlot's curse
Blasts the new-born Infant's tear
And blights with plagues the Marriage hearse.

Proverb II
Prisons are built with stones of Law, Brothels
  with bricks of Religion.

THE CHIMNEY-SWEEPER

A little black thing among the snow,
Crying 'weep 'weep in notes of woe!
Where are thy father and mother? say?
They are both gone up to the church to pray.

Because I was happy upon the heath,
And smil'd among the winter's snow
They clothed me in the clothes of death,
And taught me to sing the notes of woe.

And because I am happy & dance & sing
They think they have done me no injury,
And are gone to praise God & his Priest & King
Who make up a heaven of our misery.

Proverb III
The bird a nest, the spider a web, man friendship.

A POISON TREE

I was angry with my friend:
I told my wrath, my wrath did end.
I was angry with my foe:
I told it not, my wrath did grow.

And I water'd it in fears,
Night & morning with my tears;
And I sunned it with smiles,
And with soft deceitful wiles.

And it grew both day and night,
Till it bore an apple bright.
And my foe beheld it shine,
And he knew that it was mine.

And into my garden stole
When the night had veil'd the pole,
In the morning glad I see
My foe outstretch'd beneath the tree.

Proverb IV
Think in the morning. Act in the noon. Eat in
  the evening. Sleep in the night.

THE TYGER

Tyger! Tyger! burning bright
In the forests of the night:
What immortal hand or eye
Could frame thy fearful symmetry?

In what distant deeps or skies
Burnt the fire of thine eyes?
On what wings dare he aspire?
What the hand dare seize the fire?

And what shoulder, & what art,
Could twist the sinews of thy heart?
And when thy heart began to beat,
What dread hand? & what dread feet?

What the hammer? what the chain?
In what furnace was thy brain?
What the anvil? what dread grasp
Dare its deadly terrors clasp?

When the stars threw down their spears,
And water'd heaven with their tears,
Did he smile his work to see?
Did he who made the Lamb make thee?

Tyger! Tyger! burning bright
In the forests of the night:
What immortal hand or eye
Dare frame thy fearful symmetry?

Proverb V
The tygers of wrath are wiser than the
  horses of instruction.
If the fool would persist in his folly he
  would become wise.
If others had not been foolish, we should be so.

THE FLY

Little Fly,
Thy summer's play
My thoughtless hand
Has brush'd away.

Am not I
A fly like thee?
Or art not thou
A man like me?

For I dance
And drink & sing:
Till some blind hand
Shall brush my wing.

If thought is life
And strength & breath
And the want
Of thought is death;

Then am I
A happy fly,
If I live,
Or if I die.

Proverb VI
The hours of folly are measur'd by the clock;
  but of wisdom, no clock can measure.
The busy bee has no time for sorrow.
Eternity is in love with the productions of
  time.

AH, SUN-FLOWER

Ah, Sun-flower! weary of time,
Who countest the steps of the Sun;
Seeking after that sweet golden clime,
Where the traveller's journey is done:

Where the Youth pined away with desire,
And the pale Virgin shrouded in snow,
Arise from their graves and aspire
Where my Sun-flower wishes to go.

Proverb VII
To see a World in a Grain of Sand,
And a Heaven in a Wild Flower,
Hold Infinity in the palm of your hand,
And Eternity in an hour.

EVERY NIGHT AND EVERY MORN

Every Night & every Morn
Some to Misery are Born.
Every Morn & every Night
Some are Born to sweet delight.
Some are Born to sweet delight,
Some are Born to Endless Night.
We are led to Believe a Lie
When we see not Thro' the Eye,
Which was Born in a Night, to perish in a Night,
When the Soul Slept in Beams of Light.
God Appears & God is Light
To those poor Souls who dwell in Night,
But does a Human Form Display
To those who Dwell in Realms of Day.

From the Songs of Experience,
the Auguries of Innocence,
and the Proverbs of Hell,
selected by Peter Pears

NOTE

The sign ⌢ over a note or rest shows that the singer must listen and wait till the pianist has reached the next barline, or meeting point—i.e., the note or rest can be longer or shorter than its written value.

Duration: *c.* 22 minutes

The first performance of *Songs and Proverbs of William Blake* was given by Dietrich Fischer-Dieskau and Benjamin Britten at the Aldeburgh Festival, June 24th, 1965.

SONGS AND PROVERBS OF WILLIAM BLAKE

BENJAMIN BRITTEN
Op. 74

Proverb I
Recitative (broadly)

The pride of the pea-cock is the glo-ry of God. The lust of the goat is the boun-ty of God.

*See Note opposite

The wrath of the li - on is the wis - dom of God.

The na-ked-ness of wo-man is the work of God.

attacca

LONDON
Very agitated (♩=88)

I wan - - der thro' each char - ter'd street,

* 𝄢 = an octave lower than written, until 𝄢, then loco. See also p.7.

Near where the char-ter'd Thames___ does___ flow

And mark___ in ev-'ry face_____ I meet___

Marks of weak-ness, marks___ of___ woe.

In ev-__-'ry cry___ of ev-__-'ry Man,

In ev - - 'ry In - fant's cry of fear,

In ev - 'ry voice, in ev - 'ry ban,

The mind - forg'd ma - na - cles I hear.

How the Chim - ney - sweep - er's cry

Ev - 'ry black-'ning Church____ ap - palls, And____ the hap - less Sol - - - dier's sigh Runs in blood down Pa - - - lace walls. But most_____ thro' mid - night streets I hear How the youth - ful Har - lot's

curse Blasts___ the new-born In - fant's tear, the

new - born___ In - - fant's tear

And blights___ with plagues___ the Mar - riage hearse.

attacca

Proverb II

As at the start (own tempo) *f*

Pri-sons are built with stones of Law,

ppp

f regular dim.

Ped.

p ⌐3¬

Bro-thels with bricks of Re-li-gion.

p

pp

Ped.

attacca

THE CHIMNEY-SWEEPER
Rather slow, cold (♩. = 50)

p clearly

mf

dim.

✳ (*pochiss. Ped.*)

lightly

A lit-tle black thing a-mong the

pp

✳ 𝄢⁸ = an octave higher than written, until 𝄞, then *loco.*

They think— they have done me no in - ju-ry,—

And are gone to praise God and— his Priest and King

Who make up a hea - ven— of our

mi - se-ry.—

attacca

Proverb III

As at the start

A POISON TREE

Slow and solemn (♩=48)
(*little movement*)

I was an-gry___ with my friend: I told my wrath, my wrath did end.

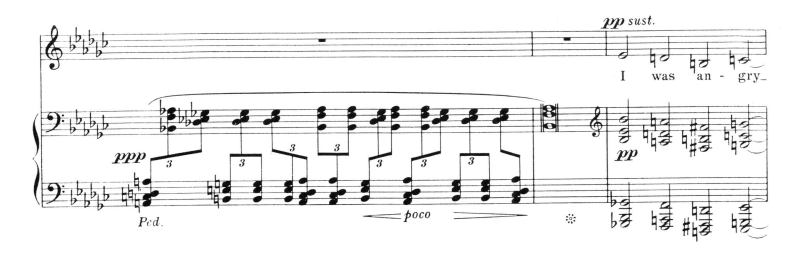

I was an-gry___

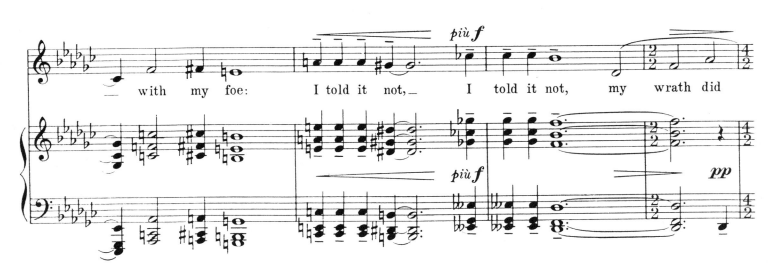

with my foe: I told it not,___ I told it not, my wrath did

And with soft de-ceit-ful wiles, with soft de-ceit-ful wiles.

(My wrath did grow.)

And_ it grew both_ day_ and night, Till it_ bore an ap-ple_ bright,

an ap-ple_ bright. And my foe be-held it shine, And he

Proverb IV

As at the start

THE TYGER

What im - mor - tal hand or eye_____ Could

frame thy fear - ful sym-me-try?_____

In what dis - - tant deeps or skies Burnt the fire____

of thine eyes? On what wings dare he as - pire?

What the hand dare seize the fire?_____ And what shoul-der,

and what art,_____ Could_ twist the sin-ews of thy heart?_

And_____ when thy heart be-

-gan to beat, What dread hand? and what dread feet? What the ham-mer?

what the chain?___ In what fur - nace___ was thy brain?_____ What the

an - vil? what dread grasp Dare___ its dead - ly ter-rors

clasp?_____ When the stars___

threw down their spears, And wa - ter'd hea-ven with their

What im-mor - tal hand or eye_____ Dare___

frame thy fear - ful sym - me - try?_____

attacca

Proverb V

As at the start

The ty-gers of wrath

f regular

are wis - er___ than the hor - ses of in - struc - tion.

If the fool___ would per-sist in his fol - ly he would be - come_ wise.

If oth-ers had not been fool-ish, we should be_ so.___

THE FLY

Moderately quick (♩=92)

Lit-tle Fly, lit-tle Fly,

Thy sum-mer's play My thought-less hand

Has brush'd a - way.

(senza Ped.)

attacca

Proverb VI
As at the start

(own tempo)

The hours____ of fol - ly   are mea - sur'd by the clock;

pp

rather heavy

repeat ad lib.

but of wis - dom,   no clock   can   mea - sure.____

The bu - sy bee   has   no time for sor - row.____

mp

mf

E-ter-ni-ty_____ is in love_____ with the pro-duc-tions of

time._____

rall. - - -

attacca subito

AH! SUN-FLOWER

Slow March (♩=52-56)

Ah,_____

The bass always heavy

pp *(sempre con Ped.)* *cresc. molto*

*Grace notes *on* the beat.

Proverb VII

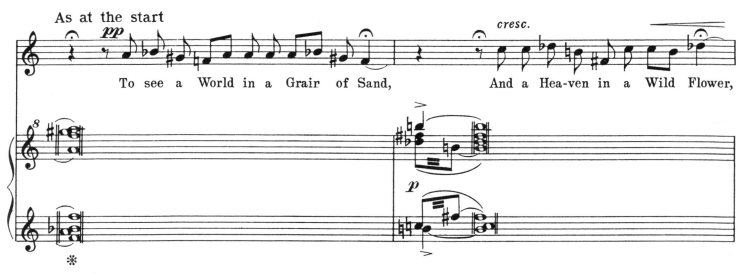

To see a World in a Grair of Sand,　　And a Hea-ven in a Wild Flower,

Hold— In-fin-i-ty in the palm of your hand,　　And E-

-ter-ni-ty in an hour.

EVERY NIGHT AND EVERY MORN

Gently moving (♩=73)

pp very smooth

con Ped.

dim.
God is Light To those poor Souls who dwell in
dim.
Night,
p
But does a Hu - man Form Dis -
p
-play
To those who Dwell in Realms of Day.
dim.
rall. very slow
expressive
ppp

Aldeburgh
April 6th 1965